Guinea Pigs

Dash!
LEVELED READERS
An Imprint of Abdo Zoom • abdobooks.com

1

Dash!
LEVELED READERS

Level 1 – Beginning
Short and simple sentences with familiar words or patterns for children who are beginning to understand how letters and sounds go together.

Level 2 – Emerging
Longer words and sentences with more complex language patterns for readers who are practicing common words and letter sounds.

Level 3 – Transitional
More developed language and vocabulary for readers who are becoming more independent.

abdobooks.com

Published by Abdo Zoom, a division of ABDO, PO Box 398166, Minneapolis, Minnesota 55439.
Copyright © 2019 by Abdo Consulting Group, Inc. International copyrights reserved in all countries.
No part of this book may be reproduced in any form without written permission from the publisher.
Dash!™ is a trademark and logo of Abdo Zoom.

Printed in the United States of America, North Mankato, Minnesota.
092018
012019

Photo Credits: iStock, Shutterstock
Production Contributors: Kenny Abdo, Jennie Forsberg, Grace Hansen, John Hansen
Design Contributors: Dorothy Toth, Neil Klinepier

Library of Congress Control Number: 2018945714

Publisher's Cataloging in Publication Data

Names: Murray, Julie, author.
Title: Guinea pigs / by Julie Murray.
Description: Minneapolis, Minnesota : Abdo Zoom, 2019 | Series: Pet care |
    Includes online resources and index.
Identifiers: ISBN 9781532125232 (lib. bdg.) | ISBN 9781641856683 (pbk.) |
    ISBN 9781532126253 (ebook) | ISBN 9781532126765 (Read-to-me ebook)
Subjects: LCSH: Guinea pigs as pets--Juvenile literature. | Guinea pigs--Behavior--
    Juvenile literature. | Pets--Juvenile literature. | Guinea pigs--Juvenile literature.
Classification: DDC 636.935--dc23

Table of Contents

Guinea Pigs

Guinea pigs make great pets.
They are calm and friendly.
Ella holds her guinea pig.

Guinea pigs are **social** animals.
They should not live alone.

Guinea pigs need a large cage.
It needs to be kept clean.

The cage needs bedding. It can be torn newspaper or wood shavings.

Guinea pigs need fresh food and water every day. They eat **pellets** and hay. They like fruits and vegetables too.

Guinea pigs need exercise.
They like tunnels and ramps.
They also like places to hide.

15

Guinea pigs need wooden toys to chew. These keep their teeth from growing too long.

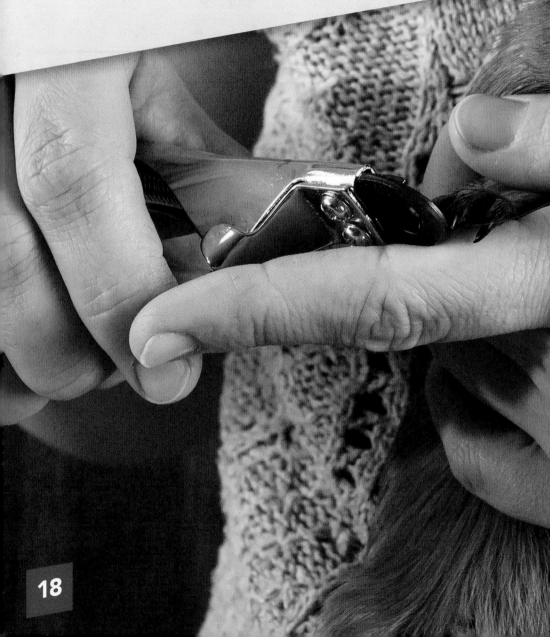

Guinea pigs need **grooming**.
They like to be brushed softly.
Kate carefully trims Honey's
nails.

Guinea pigs like to be held and cuddled. John loves his guinea pig.

Things Guinea Pigs Need

- Fresh food and water

- A cage with bedding

- Tunnels and ramps for exercise

- Wooden chew toys for teeth

Glossary

groom – to make clean and neat.

pellet – a small rounded mass of food.

social – living in groups of communities instead of alone.

Index

Online Resources

Booklinks
NONFICTION NETWORK
FREE! ONLINE NONFICTION RESOURCES

To learn more about guinea pig care, please vis **5**
abdobooklinks.com. These links are routinely
monitored and updated to provide the most currᴇɴᴛ
information available.